Read All About Numbers

NUMBERS AND MEASURING

John M. Patten, Jr., Ed.D.

The Rourke Corporation, Inc.
Vero Beach, Florida 32964

John M. Patten, Jr. Ed.D.
25 years of professional experience as a writer, elementary and secondary school teacher, elementary school principal and K-12 system wide director of curriculum.
        B.A.—English and social studies; M.ED.—Guidance and education; ED.D.—Education

MATH CONSULTANT:
Mrs. Barbara Westfield, M.S. — Grade Three Teacher

PHOTO CREDITS
Cover, pages 13, 16, 18, 19, 21, 22 © John Patten; pages 4, 6, 7, 9, 10, 15 © Zack Thomas; page 12 © N. Hood

Library of Congress Cataloging-in-Publication Data

Patten, J. M., 1944-
    Numbers and measuring / by John M. Patten, Jr.
        p. cm. — (Read all about numbers)
    Includes index.
    Summary: Discusses the inch-pound system used in the United States to measure size, weight, height, and distance and the metric system used for the same purposes elsewhere.
    ISBN 0-86593-434-7
    1. Mensuration—Juvenile literature. [1. Measurement.]
I. Title II. Series: Patten, J. M., 1944-   Read all about numbers
QA465.P35 1996
530.8'1—dc20
                                                        96–12626
                                                            CIP
                                                            AC

Printed in the USA

TABLE OF CONTENTS

TWO WAYS PEOPLE MEASURE

People **measure** (MEHZH er) real, or touchable, things with official **number units** (NUM ber YU nitz), or amounts. These units of measurement are not the same everywhere in the world.

In the United States, the **inch-pound system** (INCH POWND SIS tem), or way of measuring, is commonly used. In almost all other countries of the world, people use the **metric system** (MET rik SIS tem) of measurement.

Let's read about these different **units** (YU nitz) of measurement. Maybe you'll find a new favorite.

These guys are up in the air about which measurement system they favor.

WHAT IS MEASURING?

How tall are you? How far is London from New York? How heavy is that sack of potatoes? How much soda pop comes in a can? People measure or have already measured to find the answers to these questions.

By measuring, people find out things like **size** (SIZE), amount, weight, height and distance. This kind of information helps us buy food and clothes, build things and even plan trips.

These boys need to measure to find out who is taller.

Did you learn to tell time on a clock like this?

Some other important measuring is done by useful instruments. Clocks, for example, tell time; calculators do arithmetic; and **thermometers** (ther MOM eh terz) measure temperatures.

Many things have already been measured. We know the distance from New York to London; and, because it won't change, it need not be measured again. Can you think of other things that have already been measured?

LENGTH IN THE INCH-POUND SYSTEM

Length (LENGKTH) is how long a thing is from end to end. Length can also be called the distance between two places. **Height** (HITE) is how tall a person is or how high something goes.

In the inch-pound system, length, distance and height are measured this way:

12 inches = 1 foot

3 feet = 1 yard

5,280 feet = 1 mile

Shorter lengths are measured in inches, feet and yards. Distances and great heights are measured in miles.

Is a foot still a foot when it is not 12 inches?

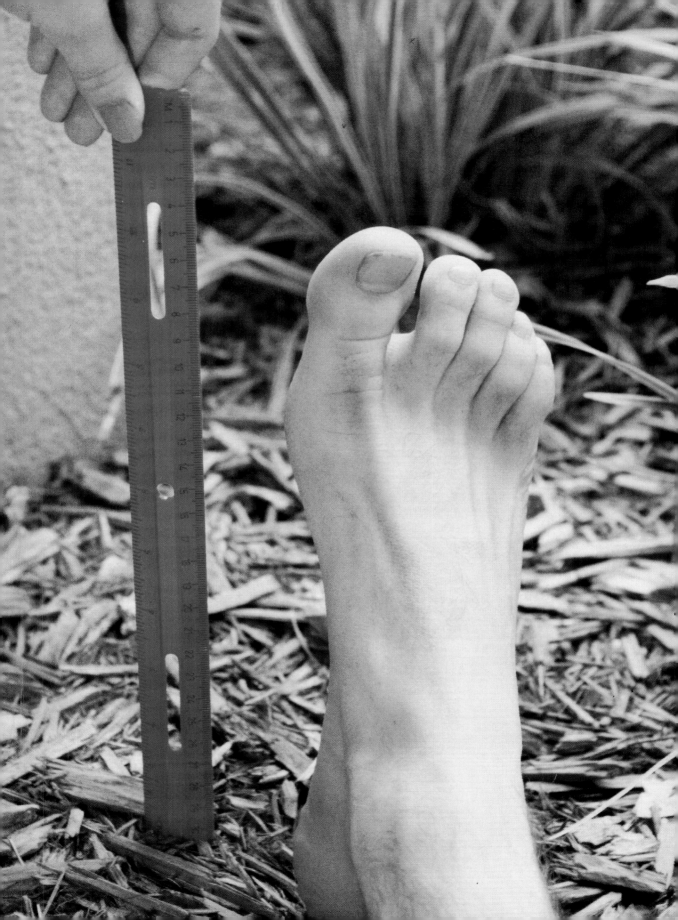

HOW ABOUT WEIGHT?

Weight (WAYT) is commonly known as how heavy an object is. Maybe our bag of potatoes weighs about five pounds.

In the inch-pound system, weight is measured in units called ounces, pounds and tons:

16 ounces = 1 pound

2,000 pounds = 1 ton

Packages of cereal and chips are usually marked in ounces. Pounds are the most common measure of weight. Planes, trucks, trains and ships are weighed in tons.

The equipment used in heavy construction weighs tons.

FLUID OR LIQUID MEASURE

The following are the units of measure for fluids, or liquids, in the inch-pound system.

8 fluid ounces = 1 cup

16 fluid ounces = 1 pint

2 pints = 1 quart

4 quarts = 1 gallon

Soda cans usually hold 12 ounces.

Water tanks like this one hold thousands of gallons.

Cans of soda pop usually contain 12 fluid ounces but are sold in both larger and smaller sizes. Milk comes in pints, quarts, half-gallons and even gallons for thirsty families.

Gasoline is sold in gallons. Swimming pools and water tanks hold thousands of gallons of water.

METRIC SYSTEM USES LIKE NUMBERS

The metric system and the inch-pound system tell time the same way. The units of measure in both are seconds, minutes and hours.

All other units of metric measure are based on 10, 100, 1,000 and so on. Adding and subtracting all these zeros should make using metrics easier.

Many people think the metric system is a simpler way to measure than our inch-pound system.

The world's scientists use the metric system. Someday, the metric system may be common in the United States.

The metric system of measure is used in the study of science.

LENGTH IN THE METRIC SYSTEM

The meter is the basic unit of length in the metric system. A meter is about the size of a yard —just over three feet.

A meter stick is marked in millimeters and centimeters. Ten millimeters equal one centimeter. Here are the units of length in the metric system used in most other countries:

10 millimeters = 1 centimeter

10 centimeters = 1 decimeter

10 decimeters = 1 meter

1,000 meters = 1 kilometer

A meter is almost 40 inches, and a kilometer is shorter than a mile.

Look closely: The car speedometer measures miles per hour with the outside numbers, and kilometers per hour with the inner ring of numbers.

METRIC WEIGHT AND LIQUID MEASURES

The gram is the basic unit of weight in the metric system. The most used metric measurements of weight are these:

    10 milligrams = 1 centigram

    10 centigrams = 1 decigram

    10 decigrams = 1 gram

    1,000 grams = 1 kilogram

About 450 grams equal one pound in the inch-pound system.

In the U.S., vegetables like these peppers are sold by the pound, not grams or kilograms.

Juice is sold by the quart, not the liter.

A metric unit for measuring liquids is the liter. Other fluid, or liquid, metric units of measurement are these:

10 milliliters = 1 centiliter

10 centiliters = 1 deciliter

10 deciliters = 1 liter

A liter is more than one quart in the inch-pound system.

IS IT THE SAME SIZE?

The units of a measuring system must be the same wherever the system is used. A quart must be the same in New York and New Mexico. A liter must be the same amount in Bangkok as it is in London.

The Bureau of Weights and Measures checks metric units of measure in countries of the world to make sure they are all the same. The Bureau even keeps an official meter stick locked in a safe in its office outside Paris, France.

In the United States, the National Institute of Standards and Technology has the job of making sure the measurement units of our inch-pound system are the same across the nation.

The United States is the only country in the world to use the inch-pound measurement system.

GLOSSARY

height (HITE) — how tall a person is or how high something goes

inch-pound system (INCH POWND SIS tem) — way of measuring used in the United States

length (LENGKTH) — how long something is from end to end

measure (MEHZH er) — to learn the size or amount of

metric system (MET rik SIS tem) — way of measuring used in most countries

number units (NUM ber YU nitz) — amounts

size (SIZE) — the measure of something, how "big" it is

thermometers (ther MOM eh terz) — instruments that tell temperature

units (YU nitz) — equal or same-sized parts

weight (WAYT) — how heavy an object is

In this flood prone area, water over the road is measured in feet.

INDEX